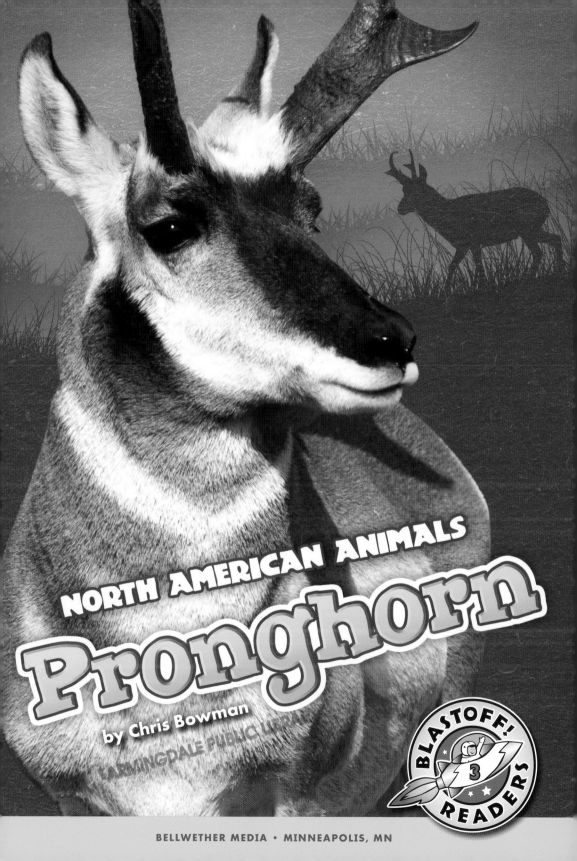

NORTH AMERICAN ANIMALS

Pronghorn

by Chris Bowman

BLASTOFF! READERS

3

BELLWETHER MEDIA • MINNEAPOLIS, MN

Note to Librarians, Teachers, and Parents:

Blastoff! Readers are carefully developed by literacy experts and combine standards-based content with developmentally appropriate text.

Level 1 provides the most support through repetition of high-frequency words, light text, predictable sentence patterns, and strong visual support.

Level 2 offers early readers a bit more challenge through varied simple sentences, increased text load, and less repetition of high-frequency words.

Level 3 advances early-fluent readers toward fluency through increased text and concept load, less reliance on visuals, longer sentences, and more literary language.

Level 4 builds reading stamina by providing more text per page, increased use of punctuation, greater variation in sentence patterns, and increasingly challenging vocabulary.

Level 5 encourages children to move from "learning to read" to "reading to learn" by providing even more text, varied writing styles, and less familiar topics.

Whichever book is right for your reader, Blastoff! Readers are the perfect books to build confidence and encourage a love of reading that will last a lifetime!

This edition first published in 2015 by Bellwether Media, Inc.

No part of this publication may be reproduced in whole or in part without written permission of the publisher. For information regarding permission, write to Bellwether Media, Inc., Attention: Permissions Department, 5357 Penn Avenue South, Minneapolis, MN 55419.

Library of Congress Cataloging-in-Publication Data

Bowman, Chris, 1990- author.
 Pronghorn / by Chris Bowman.
     pages cm. – (Blastoff! Readers. North American Animals)
 Includes bibliographical references and index.
 Summary: "Simple text and full-color photography introduce beginning readers to pronghorn. Developed by literacy experts for students in kindergarten through third grade"– Provided by publisher.
 Audience: Ages 5-8.
 Audience: K to Grade 3.
 ISBN 978-1-62617-192-3 (hardcover : alk. paper)
 1. Pronghorn–Juvenile literature. I. Title.
 QL737.U52B69 2015
 599.63'9–dc23
                                                    2014042702

Printed in the United States of America, North Mankato, MN.

Table of Contents

Pronghorn are hoofed **mammals**. They are the fastest land animals in North America!

N
W   E
S

Extinct

Extinct in the Wild

Critically Endangered

Endangered

Vulnerable

Near Threatened

Least Concern

pronghorn range =

conservation status: least concern

Most pronghorn run around the western United States. Some roam into northern Mexico and southern Canada.

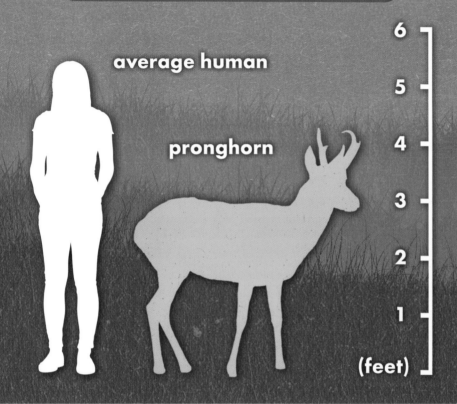

Size of a Pronghorn

average human

pronghorn

6
5
4
3
2
1
(feet)

Pronghorn look like medium-sized deer.

They stand about 3 feet (0.9 meters) tall at the shoulders. Their bodies can measure 5 feet (1.5 meters) long.

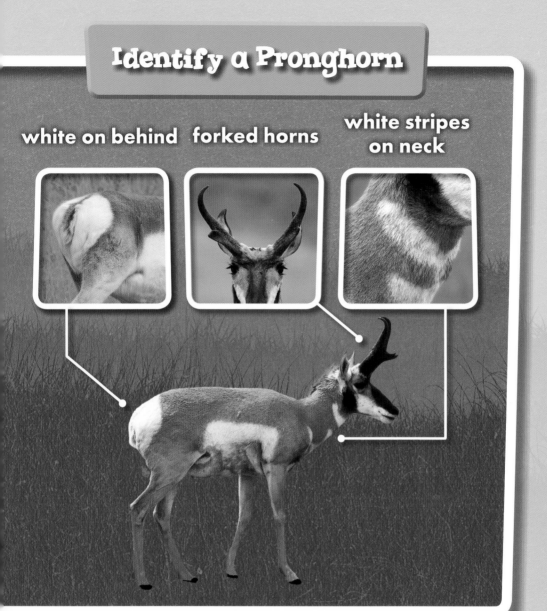

white on behind   forked horns   white stripes on neck

Reddish brown fur coats their bodies. This fur can be darker brown or tan on some pronghorn.

White fur covers their bellies
and back ends. Their necks
have white stripes.

Pronghorn are named for their forked horns. On males, these horns can grow to be more than 1 foot (30 centimeters) long. The horns of females are much shorter.

Pronghorn **shed** their horns every year like animals with **antlers** do. They are the only horned animals to do this.

Finding Food

Pronghorn are **herbivores**. They **forage** in prairies, **scrublands**, and deserts for grasses and other plants.

On the Menu

alfalfa

sagebrush

rabbitbrush

biscuitroot

bluegrasses

prickly pear cacti

They eat their meals twice. The second time, they chew their food as **cud**. This breaks the plants down more.

Pronghorn run long distances for food. Some **herds** travel 150 miles (241 kilometers) south every winter. They return north in spring.

The trip is one of the longest **migrations** in North America.

Pronghorn can spot movement from 4 miles (6.4 kilometers) away! They raise the white fur on their back ends to warn others of danger. They also snort and stamp their feet.

Sometimes **predators** get close. However, pronghorn can run up to 53 miles (85 kilometers) per hour. They escape from coyotes, bobcats, and others.

Male pronghorn are called **bucks**. They guard **territories** for females, or **does**.

Sometimes bucks fight one another with their horns.

Baby Facts

Name for babies:	fawns
Size of litter:	1 to 2 fawns
Length of pregnancy:	8 months
Time spent with mom:	about 1 year

Does give birth to **fawns** in spring.
Each doe has one or two fawns.
The fawns hide in tall grass at first.
But soon they are on the run!

Glossary

antlers—branched bones on the heads' of some animals; antlers look like horns.

bucks—male pronghorn

cud—food that has been spit up to be chewed again

does—female pronghorn

fawns—baby pronghorn

forage—to go out in search of food

herbivores—animals that only eat plants

herds—groups of pronghorn that live and travel together

mammals—warm-blooded animals that have backbones and feed their young milk

migrations—trips from one place to another, often with the seasons

predators—animals that hunt other animals for food

scrublands—dry lands with short bushes and trees

shed—to lose something on the body at the same time every year; pronghorn shed their horns.

territories—areas that male pronghorn defend for females

To Learn More

AT THE LIBRARY

Bowman, Chris. *White-tailed Deer*. Minneapolis, Minn.: Bellwether Media, 2015.

Lunis, Natalie. *Pronghorn: Long-distance Runner!* New York, N.Y.: Bearport Pub., 2011.

Pero, Denis. *My Book of Animals: A Walk Through the National Parks*. Paris, Fr.: Aozou Publishing, 2013.

ON THE WEB

Learning more about pronghorn is as easy as 1, 2, 3.

1. Go to www.factsurfer.com.

2. Enter "pronghorn" into the search box.

3. Click the "Surf" button and you will see a list of related web sites.

With factsurfer.com, finding more information is just a click away.

Index

The images in this book are reproduced through the courtesy of: Donald M. Jones/ Corbis, front cover, pp. 10, 19; Tom Reichner, pp. 4-5, 8 (top center), 11; Wayne Lynch/ All Canada Photos/ SuperStock, pp. 6-7; Sarah Jessup, p. 8 (top left); Alan Scheer, p. 8 (top right); IrinaK, p. 8 (bottom); puttsk, p. 9; Fred Lord/ Alamy, p. 12; Kazakov Maksim, p. 13 (top left); Kerry V. McQuaid, p. 13 (top right); Tim Pleasant, p. 13 (center left); Lupa, p. 13 (center right); Pelevina Ksinia, p. 13 (bottom left); Scisetti Alfio, p. 13 (bottom right); Terry Eggers/ Corbis, pp. 14-15; Larry Ditto/ Danita Delimont/ Newscom, p. 16; McDonald Wildlife Photography/ Age Fotostock, p. 17; visceralimage, p. 18 (left); Rusty Dodson, p. 18 (right); Max Allen, p. 20; Cynthia Kidwell, p. 21.